HANDBOOK OF FAITH

HANDBOOK OF FAITH

Rev. Warren C. Biebel Jr.

Healthy Life Press
Orlando, Florida

Handbook of Faith, by Warren C. Biebel Jr.

Copyright© 2012, 2013 by Warren C. Biebel Jr. All rights reserved.

Published by Healthy Life Press
Website: www.healthylifepress.com
E-mail: info@healthylifepress.com

Most Healthy Life Press products are available through quality bookstores everywhere, including major online book retailers. Copies of this book and a downloadable e-book version (or both versions packaged together at a discount) are available directly from the publisher. E-mail: info@healthylifepress.com for information. To arrange quantity discounts or learn of other special offers, please visit our website: www.healthylifepress.com or e-mail us at: info@healthylifepress.com.

This book may not be reproduced, transmitted, or stored in whole or in part by any means, including graphic, electronic, or mechanical without the express written consent of the publisher except in the case of brief quotations embodied in critical articles and reviews.

Cover Design - Healthy Life Press
Cover Image - (c) Jgroup | Dreamstime.com
Internal Design - Healthy Life Press

Library of Congress Cataloging-in-Publication Data

Biebel, Warren C., Jr.
 Handbook of Faith

ISBN 978-1-939267-20-7

1. Apologetics, 2. Biblical Studies

Third edition, 2013. Printed in the United States of America.

Undesignated Scripture references are taken from the New King James Version, copyright © 1982 by Thomas Nelson, Inc. Used by permission. All rights reserved. Certain capitalizations have been added as required by the publisher's style guide.

From the Publisher

It is always a privilege to serve one's father while we both try to serve our Heavenly Father, together. My dad, whose fourth book this is, has been the North Star of my faith since day one when he prayed me past those initial days in the incubator when my life hung into the balance until now, when at age eighty-two, he's still trying to make a difference for the Kingdom of God.

Both of us often wonder why, if there are so many so-called "Christians" in our world, we are, collectively relatively ineffective as **light** in the darkness (by comparison with the original disciples) or even as a preserving agent (as "*salt*" should be) in relation to truth, justice, and things that are good and right.

In this short book, Dad hits the nail right on the head. The sad fact is, while there may be millions of Bibles in homes worldwide, they are mostly gathering dust. Very few Christians know what the Word of God actually says, much less how it still so remarkably relates to life, day-by-day. This is partly a failure of the church, which can seem more a place of entertainment center week after week, and partly due to secondary theological concerns that continue to spawn new "denominations." But the fact remains that the Word of God is His love letter to His children, and that the quality of our faith depends on reading, understanding, believing, and practicing what it says.

INTRODUCTION

In these chaotic times, it is especially important to our lives that we have a real living faith, one that encompasses every facet of our everyday life, and that is what this little "handbook" is about. But we must begin by admitting that as Christians we don't have infinite knowledge and that many of life's questions are left unanswered.

Isaiah the prophet spoke of this when contemplating the issues swirling about him, "'For My thoughts are not your thoughts, nor are your ways My ways,'" says the Lord" (Isa. 55:8).

The apostle Paul wrote that we see only partially as in a cracked and dirty mirror (1 Cor. 13:12). He also referred in the letter to the Colossians in regard to the deity of Christ as "a mystery"! So what do these verses mean? They mean that our commitment to Jesus Christ as Lord and Savior is really based on an act or faith on our part. The part that the secular world does not understand is that having that faith is a living reality in our lives confirmed by our personal experiences with God, that unbelievers cannot share.

Faith itself is God's gracious gift to us, as Ephesians 2:8-9 says, "For by grace you have been saved through faith, and that not of yourselves; it is the gift of God, not of works, lest anyone should boast."

The 2011 *New York Times* "World Almanac" identifies among the world population of about seven billion that there are two billion, two hundred thousand who identify themselves as Christians. Its simple definition of "Christian" is "followers of Christ." There is, however, a big "But!" in this statistic. The "but" is, "But . . . how may of those included in this generality really believe in the Bible as an inspired message from God? Because " . . . faith comes by hearing, and hearing by the Word of God" (Rom. 10:17).

That leads to a second question, to which many known as "Christians" today have no really good answer: "Is the Bible really a special message from God and can we trust it?"

If it is, then it is of the greatest importance to everyone. If not, it matters little more than other kinds of wisdom literature compiled throughout the ages.

The apostle John expressed it this way toward

the end of the Gospel that bears his name, ". . . but these (these Scriptures) are written that you may believe that Jesus is the Christ, the Son of God, and that believing you may have life [spiritual life] in His name" (John 20:31).

Untold volumes have been written about the Bible, but for most ordinary people it is a book that is really unknown and not very well understood.

Faith, belief, spiritual life - all three of these essential parts of real Christianity hinge on the question, "Can we trust that the Bible is really God's own unique message to mankind?" This is a basic question that every follower of Christ should be able to answer!

– Rev. Warren C. Biebel Jr.
  Easter 2012

Contents

Introduction v

Can You Trust the Bible? 3
    Three Positions 4
    Three Tests 7
    The Witnesses 8
    The Science 10
    The Element of Faith 13

Three Historical Events 15
    Noah and the Great Flood 19
    The Exodus 23
    Jonah and the Great Fish 33

Modern Miracles 41
The Redemption of Humanity 43
The Redeemer of Humanity 45
Fulfillment of Prophecy 49
The Person and Work of the Holy Spirit .. 57
When Infants and Children Die 67

Conclusion 71

Healthy Life Press Resources 76

CAN YOU TRUST THE BIBLE?

Let's begin the discussion by acknowledging that there are and have been, for centuries, various schools of thought about the Bible within the general framework of what is called "Christianity." There are two extreme positions philosophically and theologically and many others leaning in one direction or another. Some others in their understanding of Christianity consider tradition to be of equal or more important than the Bible. Many of these people, although identified as "Christian" by label, not only do not believe in the "Jesus" of the Bible but adapt their own beliefs to a position that is socially and politically acceptable.

Three Positions

The first position is that of the theological "left," or extreme "liberal," which rejects the Bible as any "special" revelation of God. To this school of thought, the Bible contains some elements of value and some accounts that may be historically true. However, the test applied to the historical accuracy of the accounts is that of "reasonableness within the context of scientific knowledge and human experience." In simple terms, anything that is "extra-experiential" or "supernatural" cannot be believed or is relegated to the category of folklore.

Without going into all the ramifications of this belief, it obviously casts doubt on many of the accounts of Scripture and in effect, strikes at the very heart and roots of our Christian faith. Thus, it relegates Christianity to the spiritual level of every other religion in the world and makes Jesus Christ Himself a mere man,and the Bible, if used at all, as simply another resource for finding bits and parcels of truth.

Secondly, there is another position within the billions of self-professed Christians, which might be called a position of "relativity." This perspective insists that we must apply the test of human experience to accounts reported in the Bible as actually having happened. Thus, they believe that many of the accounts of historical events are fables or fictionalized (i.e. they did not really happen as described) though they may contain some valuable lessons.

The third position is called by a variety of names including "fundamentalist," "conservative," or "evangelical." In today's world, the first two unfortunately have taken on a dramatic and misleading definition. The word "fundamentalist" is being associated with "Islamic fundamentalism," which is of course untrue and unfair. Every Christian, although not necessarily embracing the title "fundamentalist," believes in the "fundamental" truth of our faith. The word "conservative" has become a political definition and confuses the issue of faith and politics. The word "evangelical," is often confused with the word "evangelist," and identified with famous people like Billy Graham, who go out and "evangelize" or try to convince people to become followers of Christ.

In general, this third group really does strive to follow Christ, regardless what name, if any, they associate with. Their basic belief is that in its original form, the manuscripts that constitute our Bible today were written by men of God who by special "inspiration" of the Holy Spirit transmitted

Almighty God's message to the human family.

It is my belief too, that the Bible that we hold and read today is a faithful rendition of those original writings and that they are without error either in content or meaning, and the only trustworthy guide for issues of faith and life.

Of course, evangelical scholars don't just accept the Scriptures without any tests. Throughout the ages, they have employed many methods of evaluating the reliability of the texts that have been passed down within the broader context of the Judeo-Christian tradition, as well as those that have been so well preserved from the earliest days of Christianity.

These scholars have applied numerous, strict tests to the Scriptures to determine their reliability, for on that issue hangs the truth or falsity of the Christian faith. So, let's consider three of those tests.

Three Tests

The first of the three tests for us to consider is the "test of historical evidence." The second is that of "scientific reliability," and the third which is somewhat different is "the test of faith and its consequences."

We need to answer the question, "What constitutes historical evidence? In other words, how do we know for sure that certain things happened? One of the ways, legally, to determine if an event really happened is by the account of witnesses. Great emphasis is placed on witnesses in our courts today. In addition, certain tests are applied to the reliability of the witnesses. Can they be trusted to be truthful? Were they in their right minds? Is there more than one witness to the same event and, if so, is their testimony in agreement? How can these tests be considered in regard to the historical reliability of the Bible?

THE WITNESSES

In regard to other ancient non-biblical manuscripts, there are severe limitations as we go back into the annals of human recorded history. Thus, we cannot find many writings to corroborate the earliest biblical writings. In ancient history, Egyptian hieroglyphics and Babylonian cuneiform provide us with a limited amount written accounts of "other" witnesses to what transpired.

As we move into the New Testament era, more and more writings are contemporary with Jesus and the apostles. We find especially in the Greek and Roman periods, much information which bears directly on the authenticity of the Scriptures, validating that what was written then is the very same text that we can hold in our hands today.

Secondly, there is the question of the witnesses themselves - that is, the writers of the Bible. There was on their part, as well as on those who helped to authenticate the Scriptures, two common understandings. The first was that they did not see themselves as super humans in any sense of the word. They were not described in this way, they did not seek to convey that idea, nor did anyone reach that conclusion. Instead, they viewed themselves as mere men, privileged to be chosen to share God's message.

They did, however, understand that what they

wrote – although containing elements of their characters and of their environment – nevertheless contained very "special" truth revealed to them by God and meant to be delivered to mankind.

Applying the tests mentioned above to these witnesses, there can be no doubt that they were totally reliable. They were in their "right" minds – many of the writings were transcribed while they had complete freedom from duress. They were men and women of outstanding character and who were not given to delusions. They represented a cross-section of human beings of every stature – people of great wealth, others of extreme poverty, men and women of the land, and others of great scientific knowledge. For example, the author of the gospel of Luke (the most specific account of Jesus' birth) was a "medical" doctor of his time and no doubt had participated in many births.

These "witnesses" were not exempt from human sin and downfall; rather, they were keenly aware of their sinfulness and shortcomings. They did not stand to gain anything from their reports, but they did stand to lose a great deal. These people stood upon the accuracy and truthfulness of their reporting to the very death.

Thus, they were witnesses whose accounts agreed in basic content and purpose and surely provided us with a great and valid test of the historical truth of Holy Scripture.

THE SCIENCE

The second test to apply is that of "scientific reliability." We begin with the admission that the Bible is not primarily either a history or science textbook. Its historical accounts are true, but at the same time, much of human history is omitted. Although the New Testament contains amazing prophecies about science and the universe itself, that is not its main message.

But what of those things that are included? It can be said that nothing that concerns scientific truth that is reported in the Bible has been proven to be untrue! The critics often pick special "targets," but in many cases, they don't examine the actual facts but rely on hearsay or conjecture. Some of the loudest critics don't even think the Bible is worthy of their time, even though history shows that the Bible has had a profound effect on some the greatest scientists and leaders the world has ever known.

Consider for example, the "Creation Account" – not what the critics say the Bible says, but what the text actually says. It accounts for an "ice age" when it says that "darkness was on the face of the deep." That's scientific! As far as God's creation of "mankind" is concerned, no one has proven that humans are not a special species. Evolution is still a theory, even though super scientists have made every effort to change species in "extra natural" ways. Think about it – where are the millions of living examples of the changing and intermingling of species, if evolution is ongoing today? Changes within species, yes, but as for the evolution of one species to another, there is no evidence!

By the way, the book of Revelation prophesies that there will come a day when scientists will give life to an inanimate object, perhaps a dead person.

In its simplest, purest form, the Bible was considered to be valid enough to be quoted by our astronauts in the journey around the moon in 1969! A golfing friend of mine, Al Worden, commander of the space module circling the moon in 1971, wrote a wonderful book of poems about this experience. In one poem he said, "About our own planet - And all the others - One thing becomes clear - When floating 240,000 miles from home - God did it all."

Consider too, the unusual recordings of Scripture such as the words of the prophet Isaiah concerning God written some 600 years before Christ, "It is He who sits above the circle of the earth . . . " (Isa. 40:22). This was long before it was known to man that the earth was round.

Or consider the geologists who, after reading that the ark of Noah was tarred with "pitch," went to the Middle East and discovered some of the world's richest oil deposits.

Or visit in Israel now a location where a potash

mill was erected on the ancient site of Sodom and Gomorrah.

Or ponder the amazing prophecies concerning the nation of Israel, fulfilled in our own time (1948), when the dispersed Jews came back to a homeland that had not existed since the first century. In this case, the fact that Biblical prophesy was specifically fulfilled cannot be denied. Only the amazing events of World War II coming together in a miraculous way made this special event possible!

THE ELEMENT OF FAITH

The third test, which is essentially different from the others, we will call the "test of faith." Hebrews defines faith in this way, "Faith is the substance of things hoped for, the evidence of things not seen" (Heb. 11:1). What a profound statement! We freely admit that faith is something we cannot prove scientifically. Paul put it this way, ". . . the natural man does not receive the things of the Spirit of God, for they are foolishness to him . . . " (1 Cor. 2:14).

So the bottom line is that even though the availability of evidence strongly supports the reliability of the Bible, it still requires faith to believe! One of the most important of all Scriptures is this, "For without faith it is impossible to please Him, for he who comes to God *must believe that He is*, and that He is a rewarder of those who diligently seek Him" (Heb. 11:6) - italics added for emphasis. In other words, a person of faith believes that God exists, even without "scientific" proof that He exists.

Faith also confirms the evidence of things which cannot be seen. This observation is not unusual, for there are untold things in the world that we do not see, but we know are there! But what is different with faith is that when exercised, God always responds to faith by "confirming." In other words, faith grows with our understanding of the Bible and as it does our faith is confirmed. This is not a circular argument but an interwoven, interlocking spiritual law which opens the vast and wonderful domain of spiritual life to the person who seeks it, and finding it, applies it to everyday experience.

Yes, the Bible is truly the "inspired" Word of God, our only real source to show us what to believe and how to live. It is the lifeblood of Christianity! It is upon the divine combination of the written Word, the Bible, and the living Word, Jesus Christ, that we rest our case.

" . . . for prophecy never came by the will of man, but holy men of God spoke as they were moved by the Holy Spirit" (2 Peter 1:21).

THREE HISTORICAL EVENTS

Now, let's consider specific events recorded in Scripture and why we believe them to be historically true. Those that I have chosen from the Old Testament all contain the following features:

1. They are presented as an actual event;
2. They contain an element which must be regarded as "supernatural" in nature, and;
3. They were quoted, referred to, and considered to be authentic by Jesus and the New Testament writers. Thus, we have selected "The Flood," "The Exodus," and the story of "Jonah." These are often the object of scorn and unbelief on the part of skeptics, which is the very reason we are choosing them.

Before we get to the cases, however, several facts should be discussed. First, there are many accounts given to us in the Bible that do not come under attack simply because they are events common to everyone. For example, today's news media are filled with reports of floods, earthquakes, and natural phenomena of every kind.

Similar events recorded in the Bible are repudiated because it is said that they had a "supernatural" cause. Some of these involve a "happening" or circumstance which was isolated and did not in itself affect the course of history. The cleansing of Naaman the leper and the floating axe head of Elisha, and many similar events fall into this category. Many such strange phenomena happen periodically and are reported in the world today. All you have to do is read your morning newspaper, and ask yourself how such a thing could happen!

In events like this in the Bible, the writers gave witness to the occurrence and explained in most cases that the event happened as a direct result of God's intervention. These events are reported, verified, accepted as having happened, but unexplained except for the message they delivered.

These accounts are important because they really stand or fall together with the balance of Scripture. The Bible consists of sixty-six books - thirty-nine in the Old Testament and twenty-seven in the New Testament. They were written over a period of several thousand years by many writers. They include historically, many cultures, a wide range of geographical data, and observations about nations and peoples. They were guarded and meticulously kept by Rabbinical guardians throughout the centuries and then by other scholars until this very day. These sixty-six books comprising our Bible are of such a special nature that they are inextricably interwoven – containing one theme, a common view of God, man, and the world. They also contain the only deep philosophical explanation for the presence of good and evil, including their source and final disposition.

More importantly, the amazing thing is that all the instruction they deliver is adaptable to the modern world and they provide a wonderful guide for living for those who believe. It is commonplace for Christians all over the world today to experience God's intervention and answers to prayers in ways that cannot be explained!

NOAH AND THE GREAT FLOOD

For our first "special event" consideration let's look at the biblical account of Noah and the ark and the great flood. In the very recent past, millions of people around the world have had to deal with disastrous floods and sunamis, which killed thousands. Floods are not that unusual and occur naturally. However, the story of Noah is far different because the Scriptures clearly state that it came as a judgment from God upon the wickedness of world. The elements of the account include Noah and his family, animal life in general, the ark as an instrument of salvation, and other less important issues. As mentioned before, it is best to stick to the simple facts of the account.

The world of Noah is described as a world "corrupted and full of violence." Noah, by contrast, was a "just" man who "walked before God." It should be remembered that the world at that time was only thinly populated both geographically and numerically. Although a listing of the animal life taken aboard the ark is not given, Noah is portrayed as the "humane society" of his day, taking in and caring for animals, reptiles, and birds for the duration of the flood.

What about the ark! This is one of the most fantastic proofs of the truth of the account. Noah was anything but a seafaring man, probably never even having seen or experienced the sea. Yet he built, with the help of his family over many years, a ship of perfect dimensions, one the size of a modern navy cruiser – big enough to provide accommodations and supplies for those who came aboard for the period of one year, the time period given in the Bible.

The flood itself is described as "covering" the mountains (hills) of that land to a depth of fifteen cubits (twenty-three feet). This is the amount of water needed to float a ship the size of the ark. Its dimensions, using a cubit as eighteen inches, would mean the ark as described in Scripture was four hundred fifty feet in length, seventy-four feet in width, and forty-five feet in depth. Allowing for three decks, this would be a ship displacing forty to fifty thousand tons – about the size of the ill-fated German battleship Bismarck in World War II. As for the flood, it most likely came about due to unusual combinations of weather systems combining for forty days and nights of driving, pouring rain!

Summing up, the most amazing part of the account, the ark itself, really provides the greatest basis for historical validity. But our belief in it also rests upon the statements of our Lord and His apostles as we an see in the following selected quotations. Jesus said, "But as it was in the days of Noah, so it will be also the days of the Son of Man.

For as in the days that were before the flood, they were eating and drinking, marrying and giving in marriage, until the day that Noah entered the ark, and did not know until the flood came and took them all away, so shall the coming of the Son of Man be" (Matthew 24:37-39). It is clear from this text that Jesus considered the flood to be an actual historical event. And He connected it with a future promised event of history yet to take place – His second coming!

Peter added in his letter to the churches this: ". . . the Divine longsuffering waited in the days of Noah, while the ark was being prepared, in which a few, that is, eight souls, were saved through water. . . . " Obviously, Peter assumed that the flood actually had occurred, historically speaking, because it was an illustration of God's saving grace.

The point of the New Testament references to the flood is that while it brought judgment on the violence and wickedness of that world, God's intervention through Noah saved the human family and gave it a fresh start. The dove of peace and the rainbow of hope put the finishing touches on what was assumed to be a true story.

Yes, we believe that Noah really lived, that the flood really happened, that the ark was miraculously planned and humanly constructed and that the purpose of God was achieved through it all.

We cannot stress enough the importance of Jesus' affirmation of the Old Testament accounts both in His beliefs and in His teaching.

Those who cannot or will not accept them in their entirety must answer this burning question: Did Jesus have, in fact, a special knowledge and understanding of the unfolding of human history and of the sacred Scriptures?

If not, then Jesus was a sincere but naive man with a distorted view of world history.

If so, Jesus knew all about the written Word because He participated in its writing. In our study, we always come back to Him (Jesus Christ) because He is the Person who provides the theme of the Bible from beginning to end.

To conclude this part of our study we refer again to the statement of Peter, for he states that the account of Noah and the ark provides us with a historical illustration of the effect of salvation through faith in Jesus, the Christ.

Here is what he says, ". . . that, by the way, is what baptism pictures for us; in baptism we show that we have been saved from doom and death by the resurrection of Christ" (1 Peter 3:21 (Phillips translation).

THE EXODUS FROM EGYPT

Now, let's consider perhaps the most important account of biblical history that is indisputable. Not only did it change the course of ancient history, but it is critical to an understanding of current events in the Middle East today. It is what we refer to as the "Exodus" or the "going out" of Egypt by the Israelites, and their wilderness wanderings and final entrance into the land of Canaan.

These events, which had their beginning in early biblical times, are continuing to unfold before our very eyes today!

The struggle being waged on the world stage today between Israel and the surrounding Arab nations had its roots in the common ancestry of these people. The issue revolves around their claim to ownership of the land. Both Jews and Arabs are descendents of Abraham, and both lay claim to the land originally promised and later possessed by him.

According to the Bible, Abraham and his lawful wife, Sarah, did not have any children and as they progressed toward old age they became more and more apprehensive about this matter. According to the custom of the time and with the consent of Sarah, Abraham took another woman, Hagar, as a "handmaid" in order that she might bear a child for him. A son was born and named Ishmael and was actually Abraham's firstborn son and, as such, the rightful heir to his birthright.

This relationship proved to be unsatisfactory to both Abraham and Sarah. As a result, Hagar and Ishmael were "banished" from the land and Ishmael became the father of the Arab nations. Just on the basis of this historical event, it is easy to understand why there is such an issue of "land ownership" in that area today.

Subsequently, another son was miraculously born to Abraham and Sarah in their advanced age, one who had been promised by God. His name was Isaac and he in turn had a son named Jacob, which was later changed to "Israel." Although the Jews and Arabs both claim a common ancestor in Abraham, and thus ownership of the land of Canaan, the dispute arises over the technicalities of who was the rightful heir of Abraham

Even today, we cannot foresee the outcome of this struggle, but we do know that prophecies in the New Testament speak of terrible events that will occur in that area in the end times which will affect the whole world. As we write, Iran continues to develop nuclear weapons and the whole Arab world is in a state of revolution and unrest and only God knows the rest of the story.

But our historical focus is the "exodus," which had its roots in the account of Joseph (a son of Jacob) being sold into slavery by his jealous brothers. After being sold, Joseph was taken by caravan into Egypt. Following a series of events which included human wisdom on his part and God's direct intervention, Joseph was afforded a position equivalent to a modern day prime minister in the Egyptian government, a very powerful status.

A sidelight of particular interest historically is that the terms and descriptions used in the biblical account are in complete "harmony" with Egyptian records of the same period. As examples, "captain of the guard," "chief of butlers," and "chief of bakers" are terms common in Egyptian terminology. As a Semite, Joseph wore a beard, but when he appeared before the court in the presence of his brothers, he was clean shaven in accordance with Egyptian customs.

According to the Bible, during a period of prolonged drought in Canaan, Joseph arranged to have his family come to live in Egypt. The account indicates that about eighty people were involved when the family moved to take up their residence in Egypt. For a long period of years, as long as Joseph's influence in the government continued, the Pharaohs looked with favor upon the Israelites. However, there came a time when the prosperity and non-integration characteristics of the Israelites became a matter of growing jealously and contention on the part of the Egyptians. Relations between the "native" Egyptians and the "Jews" continued to worsen, and finally there came and open rift which resulted in the subjugation and bondage of the Jews. They were then forcibly employed as slaves in many of the great building projects of Egypt. They were used in the making of bricks and in the construction of the pyramids as well as other Egyptian projects.

In the approximately 400 years of their residence in Egypt, the Israelites had grown in number to 600,000 men, plus women and children, a nation within a nation! This frustrated the Pharaoh in his attempt to downgrade the Israelites as a separate people and he saw them as a growing threat to the internal security of Egypt.

As a result, he ordered that all the male children of the Jews be put to death. It is at this precise moment that one of the most important figures of ancient history was born and as a male child he was to be put to death. That did not happen, because his parents put him in a basket and hid him in the bulrushes, once again showing how God oversees all things in human affairs.

Discovered by the Pharaoh's daughter and brought to the palace, Moses grew up with great cultural advantages and was educated in the very palace and accepted as a member of the royal family. These opportunities no doubt helped make it possible for Moses to be the writer of those unique and wonderful writings that constitute the first five books of our Bible, called the "Pentateuch"!

According to the "census" account given in the book of Numbers, during the 400 years of residence in Egypt, the number of Israelites had grown to 600,000 men, plus women and children. To get this number of people with their animals, possessions and supplies out of slavery and out of Egypt truly required not just one, but many special interventions by God. The fact that this event actually happened is uncontested by historians, even though they may deny that actions by God accomplished it. In my view, it takes more imagination to deny the facts of the story than it does to simply accept them as described.

In order to see things as they really happened, we must consider the parts of the Exodus account which we might call "the direct interventions of God." God felt it necessary to bring judgment upon the Egyptians because of their polytheistic beliefs and for the cruel and inhuman way they treated the Israelites and even their own people. As far as the time and environment was concerned, none of the judgments or "plagues" mentioned in the biblical record would be miraculous except the sparing of the Israelites as a result of the tenth and last plague. What made the this one supernatural was its timing, the severity of it, and most importantly, the predicted purpose to force an unwilling Pharaoh to release the Israelites.

In addition, the last plague (the death of the firstborn Egyptians) introduced an event that is kept to this very day by Jews – "The Passover." The original "passover" happened when the

Jewish people were instructed to post the blood of a sacrificial lamb over their door, as a result of which the angel of the Lord, "passed over," their house that deadly night.

Today, this event is significant not only in Jewish worship but in the Christian worship, as well. It is our belief that the sacrifice and sprinkling of the blood on the door posts as an act of obedience and faith is central to and consistent with the idea of "salvation" through Christ's sacrifice as "the Lamb of God," a theme that is carried through in the Bible from beginning to end. For example, when John the Baptist baptized Jesus, he proclaimed, "Behold! The Lamb of God who takes away the sin of the world!"

Some of the most sacred occasions of the New Testament revolve around the events that are recorded in the book of Exodus. For example, Jesus chose the occasion of the feast of the Passover to institute the "Lord's Supper" or holy communion. Referring to it, He spoke of the "New Testament" in His blood that was shed for the remission of sins. Biblical critics find it impossible to deny the account leading up to the first "Passover," but they try to have a field day with the continuing story as it contains events that must be considered supernatural, and "supernatural" is not part of their vocabulary.

Before we consider the crossing of the Red Sea and the wilderness wanderings of the Israelites under Moses' leadership, let us see how integrated the Bible really is. For example, what did some of the New Testament writers and commentators say about these events? Well, they said a lot!

Jesus told Nicodemus, "And as Moses lifted up the serpent in the wilderness, even so must the Son of Man be lifted up, that whoever believes in Him should not perish but have eternal life" (John 3:14-15). In this passage, Jesus not only made it clear the He considered the miraculous deliverance of those who in obedience looked upon the uplifted brazen serpent to be historical, but He viewed it as symbolic to His own death upon the cross!

In the book of Acts, chapter 7, Stephen, just prior to his martyrdom, reminded the Sanhedrin of the events in the books of Genesis and Exodus. Included in the history he recounted were: Moses being trained and educated according to the cultural advantages of Egypt (vs. 22), the "burning bush" (vs. 30), the plagues, and the crossing of the Red Sea (vs. 36).

In 1 Corinthians 5:7, the apostle Paul wrote, "For indeed Christ, our Passover, was sacrificed for us." It is especially important to understand that Paul, a highly educated man, believed this event to be actual history and a crucial early example (a figure) related to the role of Jesus, the Christ.

So now let's consider two of the supernatural

events that happened in "The Exodus." First, the crossing of the Red Sea, a very real barrier between Egypt and the promised land, had to happen if the Israelites were to survive. It is likely that the Israelites crossed the Red Sea in an area called "the sea of reeds."

In their frantic search for an explanation to the idea of a vast number of people including infants, animals, and supplies getting away from the Egyptians who were close on their heels, the critics suggest that the "sea of reeds" was a shallow part of the sea. Even if it were, it would surely have been deep with mud, with water above the waist, maybe even quicksand. But what really happened was that as the Egyptian army approached, Moses stood on the bank of the sea and called upon the restive, fearful people to "stand still and see the salvation of the Lord."

As in many other biblical miracles, God utilized natural means to achieve His purposes. In this case, a strong east wind backed up the water and the people crossed over safely. When the Egyptian army tried to pursue, they perished in the ensuing surf. Listen to this paraphrase of portions of Moses' song about this event written in Exodus 15:1-12:

"I will sing to the Lord for He has triumphed gloriously; He threw the horsemen into the sea. Pharaoh's chariots and officers drowned in the Red

Sea. You sent a mighty wind, pushed the water into a great wave and even as they were planning to kill us, the sea covered them and they were swallowed up and were gone."

Secondly, there is what is called, "The Wilderness Wanderings." Samuel Schultz, in his classic book, *The Old Testament Speaks* says, "The passage of so great a host of people through the wilderness transcends ordinary history." To take a group of *a hundred* people on a journey through the wastes of the Sinai peninsula would require a human engineering miracle, but to assemble, feed, maintain discipline, and transport a mass of human beings and animals in that area over a period of years could only be accomplished by a direct intervention by Almighty God, which indeed, it was! And it's all written down, just the way it happened.

All this brings us back again to our original question: Can we trust the Bible? I ask, how do the critics decide what parts of the Bible to believe and what parts to discard?

The real question though is not, "Do they believe the Bible?" It really is, "Do they believe in God?"

Nicodemus, when he was still a non-believer and a devout religious leader, came to Jesus. He was attracted to Jesus because, in his own words, "no man can do these miracles except God be with him."

The miracles recorded in both the Old and New Testaments really happened, which is clear to those of us who acknowledge and accept the existence and the power and presence of Almighty God and of His Son, Jesus Christ!

Some time ago, as a pastor, I was asked to pray for the direct intervention of God to save the life of a terribly injured young man. The request was based on the promise included in the book of James that "the prayer of faith will heal the sick" and required an act of faith.

In a moment of self-examination, I had to ask myself, "Do I really believe?" After moments of intense, deeply personal self-examination, my answer was, "Lord, I believe!" The young man not only lived but went on to college and to marry.

JONAH AND THE GREAT FISH

We've considered Noah and the Exodus – now, for the third part of our study concerning "supernatural events" let's look at another favorite object of critics' scorn, "Jonah and the great fish."

Critics may scorn, but Jesus did not. In His own words, He confirmed that this event really did happen: "An evil and adulterous generation seeks after a sign, and no sign will be given to it except the sign of the prophet Jonah. For as Jonah was three days and three nights in the belly of the great fish, so will the Son of Man be three days and three nights in the heart of the earth. The men of Nineveh will rise up in the judgment with this generation and condemn it, because they repented at the preaching of Jonah; and indeed a greater than Jonah is here" (Matthew 12:39-41).

Not to believe in the historical reality of Jonah and his story would constitute a denial of the resurrection of Jesus Christ. In the above passage, He draws a number of parallels between what He calls the "sign" of the prophet Jonah and the momentous events of His own life.

Before getting into the particulars of this account, we need to ask an important question: Concerning all these events, what do they mean to me now?

According to Jesus' statement above, it is not

necessarily meritorious for us to constantly emphasize "signs" (miracles) in our Christian lives. In fact an overemphasis on seeking miracles can be wrong. Jesus told the people always seeking miracles that no special revelations or "signs" would be given, because it would not result in their belief. He went right to the heart of the matter, which can be stated as follows: Whether it be in the historical context of the Bible or in our individual Christian lives, we will not believe in the supernatural until we are totally committed to belief in Jesus Christ Himself.

Total belief in Him cannot come until we first acknowledge the truth and reality of our own and mankind's shortcomings and sins and turn in repentance to a Savior who loved us and died for us. Jesus put it this way in denying the requests of those who sought special miracles: "Though one should rise from the dead, you would not believe." Perhaps that is why Paul wrote in Romans 10:9-10, "That if you confess with our mouth the Lord Jesus and believe in your heart that God has raised Him from the dead, you will be saved."

Christians do not need to experience "special" or "unusual" ("miraculous") events to enable them to believe or even to strengthen their spiritual lives. We should believe in Jesus Christ because of Who He is and because of what He did for us on the cross! A true believer recognizes, accepts, and responds to any special event that God brings to us as normality! He does not seek continual signs, but he does rejoice in such experiences and the more he walks with God, the more his life will become enmeshed with the direct intervention of the Lord, which is miraculous in and of itself.

The fact that Jesus would refer to the story of Jonah as a comparison to the events which immediately followed His death on the cross indicates that Jonah's experience was important for several reasons. First, the experience prepared him (Jonah) spiritually as a prophet for the task which God had given him – to preach repentance to the wicked city of Nineveh. Yet, as was so often the case in the experiences of the Old Testament prophets, their experiences were intended by God to have meaning in both their own present time, and also quite often pointing to one part or another of Jesus' redeeming work as the anointed one – the Christ, to whom the Old Testament pointed.

This would be true not only of their experiences but also of their messages and their writings. In the New Testament Paul wrote, "For whatever things were written before were written for our learning, that we through the patience and comfort of the Scriptures might have hope."

The whole scheme of "signs" and "types" recorded throughout the Old Testament and referred to so often by the writers of the New Testament was designed to point the way clearly to both a need for a Savior and to the work and works of the coming Messiah. That the prophets, scholars and people were sensitive to this fact is born out by the apprehensions and anticipations of the people prior to, at the time of, and after Jesus' earthly life.'

If you just read the story of Jonah, it reads like a personal diary! The fact that Jonah received the call of God to go down to Nineveh but that he rebelled against this idea and instead bought passage on a ship going to Tarshish is humanly understandable. Nor was he the only prophet who found his particular call unpleasant to contemplate. At any rate, we find that the ensuing events as they are described are compatible with other records which describe sea experiences of that period of history. Also, other sources indicate that the wickedness and particularly the violence of the city of Nineveh was notorious in secular as well as biblical literature.

That part of the account which some find difficult to believe occurred when Jonah was cast overboard after confessing to the ship's crew that their misfortunes with the voyage was due to his presence. At this point, the Bible tells us that God prepared "a great fish," which swallowed Jonah, and that he spent three days and three nights in the stomach of the fish. There is not doubt that there have been and are whales which are large enough to have accomplished this feat. Also, there are some strikingly similar, verified stories in secular history. Nevertheless, we are again confronted with the real issue at stake here – that the Bible states that God, by direct intervention, not only caused the storm but prepared the fish to rescue Jonah and take him to his real pre-ordained destination. The real issue here is whether one can believe that Almighty God could actually do these things.

For those who deny the validity of the book of Jonah, there is another problem and that revolves around the outcome of the account. According to the story, Jonah prayed while in the fish's stomach and was then released on the shore. He went on to preach repentance to the city of Nineveh, which responded to his warnings. Under the leadership of the king, the city repented.

At this point, the account takes a strange twist, one entirely out of keeping with a fictitious adventure story. Jonah, in the midst of an amazing success, becomes angry toward God. It is precisely at this point that we become aware that the overriding message of the book of Jonah is really about God's love for mankind. God literally brought back from certain death a rebellious prophet to effect the salvation of a city. As Jesus Himself would explain to Nicodemus, "For God so loved the world that He gave His only begotten Son, that whoever believes in Him should not perish but have everlasting life."

Not long after Jesus spoke these words, God

brought Him back from the dead to effect the salvation of the whole "world." This required the greatest of all miracles – one in which we must believe if we are true Christians.

The "little" resurrection of Jonah was a miracle, but the greatest one of all came after Jesus' death on the cross. His corpse was laid in the tomb of Joseph of Arimathea, but He came forth on the third day in glorious victory – His resurrection – which is the central and pivotal event of Christianity, indeed, of human history.

And it is this event that makes the Christian life a continuing "experience" with God. Jesus said, "Most assuredly, I say to you, he who believes in Me, the works that I do he will do also; and greater works than these he will do, because I go to My Father. And whatever you ask in My name, that I will do, that the Father may be glorified in the Son. If you ask anything in My name, I will do it" (John 14:12-14).

To sum up this portion of our "faith" study, think deeply about all that we have written. Many scholars have made very convincing arguments about the "unity" of the Bible. Much has been written about the consistency of the literary style and the harmony of its symbolism and typology. This kind of "unity" goes infinitely above what could be expected in writings contributed by many different authors over thousands of years.

Yet, towering above even these considerations

are two mountain peaks of truth affirming the Bible's amazing unity and even these merge into one message!

MODERN MIRACLES

Before we totally leave our thoughts about Jonah however, consider with me two events (of many) that dramatically changed the course of World War II. The first was the remarkable sinking of the great Nazi battleship, Bismark! This ship was commissioned by Hitler to be powerful enough to destroy anything on the high seas including Britain's entire navy and the convoys bringing desperately needed supplies and weapons to that beleaguered nation.

In its first battle, the Bismark sank the HMS Hood, the flagship and pride of the English navy, with one salvo of its huge cannons. This brought a sense of despair and depression to all of England at a truly dark moment of human history! Could anything stop this ship?

Shadowing the Bismark were many smaller ships of the British navy, including an aircraft carrier which launched twelve two-wing torpedo planes, each carrying one torpedo. Their mission was to try to sink the Bismark. They failed in the first attempt, but with great courage they tried again, approaching the ship though a rain of anti-aircraft fire. All but one of the torpedoes missed their mark but the very last one hit the only vulnerable spot on the ship, its rudder.

This so disabled the Bismark that it could not

navigate except to go in a constant circular course, which in the end led to its sinking. Was that last torpedo released by an ancient bi-plane (an event that changed the course of the war) a miracle? Many of those involved thought so!

Also in World War II, in the battle of Midway, the U.S. navy was outgunned by the Japanese fleet and had to depend on the element of surprise to even have a chance in what would be the key battle of the Pacific war with Japan. If our fleet, in inferior numbers, was discovered and destroyed the whole Pacific ocean would belong to the enemy. The Japanese sent out search planes to find our fleet with no success, until the last plane spotted and found the position of our fleet.

But there was an unusual problem, the radio did not work, so the pilot could not radio in the position of the U.S. fleet. The rest is history – the U.S. won the battle and this was the turning point in the Pacific war.

Was this God's intervention? I had a history professor, Dr. Hudson Armerding, later president of Wheaton College who was a commander in the navy and was at the planning meetings of the naval officers prior to the battle of Midway. He thought this was a divine intervention, and he shared that belief with us, his students.

I previously mentioned that in the world today, we sometimes see the hand of God intervening. That is why I included the two accounts above.

THE REDEMPTION OF HUMANITY

Returning to the two "mountain peaks" of the Bible, the first is the dramatic story of the "redemption" of the human family. The word redemption raises a question, "Why does the human family need to be redeemed?" It's a fair question. The answer lies in our ability to know "right from wrong," good from evil, and to understand their consequences.

Why did God in His creation of mankind allow for this? Because He sought the fellowship and worship of His creation – not the mechanical response of a robot. And to achieve this meant giving freedom to the human family to think, decide, and act. It didn't turn out too well, and it didn't take long for "sin" to enter . . . and unfortunately, it's here in abundance today.

Those who deny the need for repentance of course feel that they are not a party to sin, but they must acknowledge the presence of good and evil and they have no answer apart from the Bible as to the origin or ultimate outcome of these two forces. The Bible says that God is waiting patiently for every last soul to come to Him, but in the end, this world will be gone and a fresh new one will replace it, "wherein dwells righteousness."

In the meantime, faithful living involves what

the prophet Micah described, "And what does the LORD require of you but to do justly, to love mercy, and to walk humbly with your God?" (Micah 6:8).

Is that too much? For some, evidently it is too much, for injustice, cold-heartedness, and pride rule the day and are even exalted.

People of faith, however, know that in light of what He has done for us, these are the least He could ask.

THE REDEEMER OF HUMANITY

The second "mountain peak" of the Bible is the integrating "Person" of Scripture. In doctrinal terms, we are referring to the "Christology" of the Bible. As "redemption" and "Christology" merge in both the Old and New Testaments and climax in the gospel accounts of Jesus' life, death, and resurrection, the message of all sixty-six books comes clear!

Jesus knew His role in all of this, for He answered the critics who accused Him of coming to destroy the Old Testament religious customs with these words, "Do not think that I came to destroy the Law or the Prophets. I did not come to destroy but to fulfill. For assuredly, I say to you, till heaven and earth pass away, one jot or one tittle will by no means pass from the law till all is fulfilled" (Matt. 5:17-18)

In Psalm 40 it says: "In the scroll of the book it is written of me. I delight to do Your will, O my God, and Your law is within my heart." Martin Luther asked the question, "What book and what person?" and he answered, "The Scriptures and only one Person, Jesus Christ"!

Consider with me some of the statements of our Lord and the Apostles concerning Jesus in Scripture:

John 5:39: "You search the Scriptures, for in them you think you have eternal life; and these are they which testify of Me."

John 5:46, "For if you believed Moses, you would believe Me; for he wrote about Me."

Matthew 21:42, "Have you never read in the Scriptures: 'The stone which the builders rejected has become the chief cornerstone. This was the Lord's doing, and it is marvelous in our eyes'?"

(Jesus was referring to Psalm 118:22-23).

Mark 14:27, "All of you will be made to stumble because of Me this night, for it is written: 'I will strike the Shepherd, and the sheep will be scattered.'" (Jesus was quoting Zechariah 13:7).

Also, there are two especially appropriate texts relating to our study in the New Testament. The first concerns the occasion when the Jesus walked on the road to Emmaus with several of His disciples, after His resurrection. "Then He said to them, 'O foolish ones, and slow of heart to believe in all that the prophets have spoken! Ought not the Christ to have suffered these things and to enter into His glory?' And beginning at Moses and all the Prophets, He expounded to them in all the Scriptures the things concerning Himself" (Luke 24:25-27).

The second text describes Philip's explaining the Scriptures to the Ethiopian Eunuch, who just "happened" to be reading from Isaiah 53: "So the eunuch answered Philip and said, 'I ask you, of whom does the prophet say this, of himself or of some other man?' Then Philip opened his mouth, and beginning at this Scripture, preached Jesus to him" (Acts 8:34-35).

Yes, the apostles of our Lord clearly saw Jesus Christ in the prophecies and writings of the Old Testament. They saw Him as the Living Word of Life, which gave meaning and interpretation to the written Word of God, the Bible.

1 John 5:13 says, "These things I have written to you who believe in the name of the Son of God, that you may know that you have eternal life, and that you may continue to believe in the name of the Son of God."

FULFILLMENT OF PROPHECY

World Leaders no longer risk predictions of what will happen a year, a month, or even a week from now. Too often in the past has history disregarded what man thought and proceeded on its way! Yet the Bible precisely foretold events that would happen hundreds, even thousands, of years prior to the events themselves.

How could this be? The only reasonable answer lies in the fact that the Bible is special, as it claims to be. – God's revealed Word! The timetable of history continues to unfold before our very eyes today! Just as surely as human history pivoted on the life, death, and resurrection of Jesus, so it continues to build toward its final culmination.

Fulfilled prophecy supplies one of the greatest proof of the unity and integrity of the whole Bible. There can be no other explanation for the whole story - which is really His story. But unless we believe in prophecy fulfillment, much of the New Testament makes no sense at all.

An amazing event happened beside the Jordan River where John the Baptist was preaching repentance with baptism to a very large crowd of people including religious zealots. There was a huge response and many were baptized. John was preaching from Isaiah. In this setting, Jesus appeared publically for the first time and John exclaimed, "Behold! The Lamb of God who takes away the sin of the world! This is He of whom I said, 'After me comes a Man who is preferred before me, for He was before me.' I did not know Him; but that He should be revealed to Israel, therefore I came baptizing with water."

This passage illustrates precisely what we mean. If we believe this is a fulfilled prophecy (John's message from Isaiah) the whole scenario makes sense. Otherwise it does not. We can envision John speaking to a crowd about wonderful words written some 600 years before he was even born. How could a prophecy be more clear cut?

When John spoke of "the Lamb of God," he was referring to Isaiah 53, which is an amazing prediction of what Jesus would endure as God's sacrificial Lamb, the blood of which would cause the angel of God to "pass over" the house where the blood was on the doorposts (remember the story of the Exodus for the meaning of this):

"He has no form or comeliness;
And when we see Him,
There is no beauty that we should desire Him.
He is despised and rejected by men,
A Man of sorrows and acquainted with grief.

And we hid, as it were, our faces from Him;
He was despised, and we did not esteem Him.

Surely He has borne our griefs
And carried our sorrows;
Yet we esteemed Him stricken,
Smitten by God, and afflicted.

But He was wounded for our transgressions,
He was bruised for our iniquities;
The chastisement for our peace was upon Him,
And by His stripes we are healed.
All we like sheep have gone astray;
We have turned, every one, to his own way;
And the Lord has laid on Him the iniquity of us
    all.

He was oppressed and He was afflicted,
Yet He opened not His mouth;
He was led as a lamb to the slaughter,
And as a sheep before its shearers is silent,
So He opened not His mouth.

He was taken from prison and from judgment,
And who will declare His generation?
For He was cut off from the land of the living;
For the transgressions of My people He was
    stricken.

And they made His grave with the wicked—
But with the rich at His death,
Because He had done no violence,
Nor was any deceit in His mouth" (Isa. 53:2-9).

Here is a word by word description of the death of the Savior, written not be an observer standing at the Cross, but by one enabled by God to look, in advance, down the long corridors of time. Such a passage is indeed awe inspiring, illustrating the truth and uniqueness of God's Word.

David, the psalmist, was also inspired by God's Holy Spirit when he wrote the following in Psalm 22 (excerpted here), in which he described an experience (crucifixion) totally unknown in his day:

"My God, My God, why have You forsaken Me?
Why are You so far from helping Me,
And from the words of My groaning?

O My God, I cry in the daytime, but You do not hear;
And in the night season, and am not silent.

. . . I am a worm, and no man;
A reproach of men, and despised by the people.
All those who see Me ridicule Me;
They shoot out the lip, they shake the head, say ing, 'He trusted in the Lord, let Him rescue Him; Let Him deliver Him, since He delights in Him!"

Be not far from Me, for trouble is near;
For there is none to help.

I am poured out like water,
And all My bones are out of joint;
My heart is like wax; it has melted within Me.
My strength is dried up like a potsherd,
And My tongue clings to My jaws;
You have brought Me to the dust of death.

They pierced My hands and My feet;
I can count all My bones.
They look and stare at Me.

They divide My garments among them,
And for My clothing they cast lots"
    (Ps. 22:1-18, excerpted).

These are the prophetic words of David, the King of Israel, and author of many of the Old Testament Psalms! Yet the passage clearly and specifically describes the details of our Savior's death, in that:

1. These are the actual words that Jesus spoke while hanging on the Cross;
2. They describe His intense thirst;
3. They detail His death by crucifixion;
4. These are the exact words of the "mockers" present on the hill called Golgotha;
5. They did gamble for His clothing;
6. His bones were out of joint, from hanging on the Cross;
7. Blood and water came out when His side was

pierced.

The fact that the Old Testament prophets did not fully comprehend the significance of their writings lends additional credence to their unique character, for it is one thing for a writer to describe an event that he has witnessed or experienced, and a totally different matter to describe an event with which he has no experience and which he cannot even imagine.

The additional fact that prophecies like this inevitably focused on a coming Messiah is a central and irrefutable integrating feature of the Bible, not only the Bible of Jesus' day, but the Bible that we have now, which also contains similar very significant descriptions of events nearly 2,000 years in the future; specifically, events that we have seen and may yet see in our own lifetime.

It is fair to say that most, if not all of the doctrinally relevant as well as the "specific" incident aspects of Jesus' life were foretold in the Old Testament and fulfilled centuries later as recorded in the New Testament. In relation to this, it is again worth noting that the last Old Testament writing was about 400 years before Christ's birth, which of course makes the whole matter all that more amazing, and faith-confirming.

The table that follows is a brief overview of just a few of these prophecies, in addition to those of Isaiah 53 and Psalm 22, already mentioned:

The following references are organized by text,

prediction, and fulfillment. They are just a few of hundreds of prophecies about the Messiah that were fulfilled in Jesus:

- ❖ Genesis 3:15 – Conflict with Satan to be resolved by a man – Galatians 4:4;
- ❖ Genesis 17-18 – Through Abraham's seed, all the world would be blessed – Matthew 1:1;
- ❖ Genesis 49:10 – Messiah would descend from tribe of Judah – Luke 3:34;
- ❖ Isaiah 9:7 – Messiah would be heir to David's throne – Matt 1:1;
- ❖ Micah 5:2 – The place of Messiah's birth – Matt. 2:1;
- ❖ Daniel 9:25 – The time of Messiah's birth – Luke 2:1-2;
- ❖ Isaiah 7:14 – Messiah to be born of a virgin – Matt. 1:18;
- ❖ Jeremiah 31:15 – The massacre of the infants – Matt: 2:16;
- ❖ Zachariah 9:9 – The triumphal entry into Jerusalem – John 12:13,14;
- ❖ Psalm 41:9 – Betrayal by a friend – Mark 14:10;
- ❖ Zechariah 11:12 – Sold for 30 pieces of silver – Matt. 26:15;
- ❖ Psalm 16:10 – His resurrection – Matt. 26:9.

THE PERSON AND WORK OF THE HOLY SPIRIT

"... holy men of God spoke as they were moved by the Holy Spirit" (2 Peter 1:21). Who or what is the Holy Spirit, and what relationship does He have to the Bible? Within the Christian community today there is a tremendous emphasis on the Holy Spirit. What do we believe and why?

Let's consider what the Holy Spirit is NOT and what He DOES NOT DO! First, the ministry of the Holy Spirit did not end with the completion of Scripture (the biblical writings ended with the last verse of the Book of Revelation). The New Testament is very clear on the continuing ministry of the Holy Spirit in our lives as Christians today! Consider the following ways in which both Jesus and the apostles describe Who He is and what He does!

In Scripture, He is described as a comforter, counselor, teacher, prayer intercessor, author of the Scriptures (with Jesus). He instills power, moves in the hearts and lives of believers, convicts of sin, guarantees eternal life, and He "baptizes" believers into the Body of Christ.

As the third member of the Holy Trinity, the very first task recorded in the Bible concerning the Holy Spirit was to bring order out of a chaotic condition. The world itself at the time was described as being without form and void, with darkness on the face of the deep (probably an ice age). In other words, the Holy Spirit was involved in the completion of "creation" itself, and He gave form and beauty to the world and the universe. The Spirit of God is the ultimate source of creativity, who never participates in something that is chaotic!

The Holy Spirit is not a ghost or apparition. He is a real person - the third Person of the Holy Trinity. Although He is not visible, He surely can be felt. When Nicodemus questioned Jesus about how a person could be born again, Jesus responded and illustrated it by saying that while you can't see the wind, you surely can feel it. "That which is born of the flesh is flesh, and that which is born of the Spirit is spirit. Do not marvel that I said to you, 'You must be born again.' The wind blows where it wishes, and you hear the sound of it, but cannot tell where it comes from and where it goes. So is everyone who is born of the Spirit" (Jn. 3:6-8).

In these days of obsession with the occult, there is a real danger even for Christians to ascribe to the Spirit strange events and experiences. Perhaps the most important ministry of the Holy Spirit is to be a "guarantee" to each Christian of his or her faith. The apostle Paul wrote that the Holy Spirit bears witness with our spirits that we really are God's children (Rom. 8:16). The apostle John wrote, "And it is the Spirit who bears witness, because the Spirit is truth. For there are three that bear witness in heaven: the Father, the Word, and the Holy Spirit; and these three are one" (1 Jn. 5:7).

The Holy Spirit also seals our relationship with Jesus as our Savior; Ephesians 1:13-14 says, "In Him [Jesus] you also trusted, after you heard the word of truth, the gospel of your salvation; in whom also, having believed, you were sealed with the Holy Spirit of promise, who is the guarantee of our inheritance until the redemption of the purchased possession, to the praise of His glory."

Mistaken ideas about the Holy Spirit sometimes relate not to the power of God but to the worshipper's quest for his own power. There is a very strong scriptural warning about this, which can be found in Acts 8. Simon the sorcerer, who became a believer and witnessed the miraculous works of the apostles, wanted their power for himself, even offering to buy the power. Peter's answer to him should send a strong warning to Christians today who manipulate belief in the Holy Spirit and try to translate it into power for themselves. Peter answered "Your money perish with you, because you thought that the gift of God could be purchased with money! You have neither part nor portion in this matter, for your heart is not right in the sight of God. Repent therefore of this your wickedness, and pray God if perhaps the thought of your heart may be forgiven you. For I see that you are poisoned by bitterness and bound by iniquity" (Acts 8:20-23).

The Holy Spirit always agrees with the written Word of God, the Bible! After all, He participated in its creation. For the most part, the Holy Spirit today speaks to believers in and through the Bible. Great care must be taken in ascribing other messages to Him, as people sometimes do by claiming that "the Spirit told me," "the Spirit revealed to me," "I have been entrusted by the Spirit with a special message from God." Though it may be sometimes hard to discern sincerity from deceit, you may always rest assured that the Spirit of God will never instruct or teach His people in a way that conflicts with or is contrary to the message of the Bible, for that would be to call Himself a liar!

Even though there seems to be a great emphasis on the Holy Spirit talking to Christians today, through other believers, as authoritative or well-meaning as they may sound, I believe we must be cautious concerning this practice, especially when it relates to interpretation of the Scriptures or specific doctrines themselves.

While the Spirit of God surely can and does talk (or move) within us, His messages and "moving" is always consistent with and relates directly to the already revealed teachings of the Bible. One danger is that, given the excitement of knowing that He is constantly with us, we sometimes mistakenly want more; for example, messages about specific plans, places, and individuals.

God gave us the Scriptures, which are sufficient and complete enough to guide and direct us with the assistance of the Holy Spirit into all truth that we need to know for faith and life. However, believers often can and do feel an inner "moving" of the Spirit especially in regard to worship and service. For example, Paul related this kind of moving when teaching about giving; specifically, that one might be moved to give even more generously than one had originally intended. Even in such situations, we must try to discern between the Spirit's true leading and our own emotional response to a "wolf in sheep's clothing" who is trying to "fleece" the flock.

As soon as someone claims to have heard a new message that is inconsistent with the Bible, he opens the door to error and cultism. Joseph Smith and every other cult leader or founder has claimed to receive "special" messages from God, thus we have many para-Christian or pseudo-Christian sects and groups, some of them using the name "Christ" or "Christian" in the name of their group, while at the same time denying certain essentials that one must affirm in order to be a true follower of Christ, including His own statement that He is *the* way, *the* truth, and *the life* and that *no one* can come to the Father, except through believing in Him.

This exclusivity is an affront to the "inclusivity" that rules our day, but Jesus drew that line in the sand! *He is the only* Redeemer of the human race. The very idea of His atoning death on the Cross is an affront to unbelievers because they refuse to believe that they really need to be saved from their sins.

And then there is the matter of the resurrection. Recall the very brief statement of Paul that, "...if you confess with your mouth the Lord Jesus and believe in your heart that God has raised Him from the dead, you will be saved" (Rom. 10:9). The resurrection was not just some kind of fable; it really happened! As the pivotal event in human history, because through it the Lord overcame the power of death, the fear of which holds all mankind captive. To be a follower of Christ requires believing this "in your heart."

Sometimes people who claim to be speaking for God, and in Christ's name, will deny these central truths, thereby perverting the gospel by mixing falsehood with its simple purity and truth. The apostle Paul described such spokespersons and their just desserts with some of the strongest words in the New Testament: "...there are some who trouble you and want to pervert the gospel of Christ. But even if we, or an angel from heaven, preach any other gospel to you than what we have preached to you, let him be accursed. As we have said before, so now I say again, if anyone preaches any other gospel to you than what you have received, let him be accursed" (Gal. 1:7-9).

Thus, it behooves us to be very sensitive to what the Spirit says to us and just as sensitive to be sure it is Him speaking. This kind of discernment usually comes with time and one's in depth knowledge of the Scriptures.

Then there is what is sometimes called the "mystery" of the "filling" of the Holy Spirit. Paul warned believers to not be drunk with wine, but to be "filled with the Holy Spirit." How can a person fill our lives as Christians? Well, we know that our bodies are His "temple" and that He indwells us. But to what degree? The implication of the command to be filled is that the Holy Spirit can be present with us and guarantee our salvation, but we may not be allowing Him to control our lives – in other words, we may be retaining control of some things within ourselves. Being "filled" means being "controlled by" the Holy Spirit.

Jesus taught the parable of the seed and the sower, and in it, the final group of those who heard the Word (the planted seed) were those in whose lives the seed came alive and grew to produce good fruit. It is my deep belief that that is exactly how a Christian becomes filled with the Holy Spirit. It means receiving Him through the "new birth" and coming alive spiritually. Then, we, like the good seed in the parable begin to grow into a fuller. deeper spiritual life, one producing abundant fruit for the Lord. While no one is ever perfectly "filled with the Spirit," it is possible to be controlled and empowered by the Spirit of God to the degree that a believer chooses to understand and seek to fulfill the will of God, moment by moment, for His glory.

The gifts of the Spirit are given to us for that very purpose. There are two primary Scripture passages that deal specifically with the matters of the "gifts" of the Spirit and the filling of the Spirit – Galatians 5 and 1 Corinthians 13. These two passagess teach us that the true test of the filling of Spirit is the degree to which we produce the "fruits" or demonstrate the character qualities that are specifically listed.

The bottom line of this teaching is that anything that is said or done, even in the Name of the Lord, is worthless unless it is done in "love." Love, not public exercise of special gifts, is the context in which the gifts of the Spirit are exercised.

There may be a place in worship for the speaking in tongues or other ways to identify with a spiritual life. But even if they are done in a scriptural way, I do not feel that they demonstrate the "filling" of the Spirit as clearly as the display of the "fruits of His presence in our lives" demonstrates this. Galatians 5:22-25 reads: "But the fruit of the Spirit is love, joy, peace, longsuffering, kindness, goodness, faithfulness, gentleness, self-control. Against such there is no law. And those who are Christ's have crucified the flesh with its passions and desires. If we live in the Spirit, let us also walk in the Spirit." His point is clear enough, if you read it in the larger context of these verses. If we live "in the Spirit," and the Spirit lives in us, the primary evidence will be exhibited in God's character, in us, not in the exhibition of the special gifts.

The Holy Spirit cannot and will not "fill" a Christian's life unless it is empty of two particular things, sin and self, and in one respect these are both the same. The idea of "filling" and "control" suggest that I can give myself completely over to Him, giving Him control of my will and it is then that He can utilize me for God's glory. He can take my mind, body, and spirit and use them in an untold number of ways.

But how does all this start? With a conscious decision, which can be different for each individual. It can be a very emotional decision or as in the case of Elijah, it can be hearing and heeding the "still, small voice" of God within our own heart.

However this happens, one must not let our experience of His filling be divisive and confusing within the Body of Christ. Jesus' prayer the "they may be one even as We (the Godhead) are one" must be respected and honored. Remember, God is a God of unity, peace, truth, and order, not chaos, and all things must be done in love, to build up the Body of Christ, not to tear it down.

If we are filled with God's Spirit, we will walk in love, and demonstrate His continuing presence in our world through our love, joy, peace, longsuffering, kindness, goodness, faithfulness, gentleness, and self-control. These qualities point people to the Source, because they know that they are supernatural (not human) when practiced with consistency and grace.

WHEN INFANTS OR CHILDREN DIE

Well, we have covered a lot of ground about faith, but there is one more matter I would like to share about the eternal destiny of infants and children who have died!

In our Christian faith, death is portrayed as an "enemy." It is easy to see why, when we see death all around us in the world. Every day we read of accidents, tornadoes, wars, crimes and every kind of event that takes away loved ones. These bring sorrow and despair to families and individuals when they touch our lives in a personal way.

I do not presume to know the "why" of this, and I don't think anyone else does, either. However, I do know that there is a special comfort available to us through our faith in Jesus Christ. It was Jesus who had much to say about children and it was to His words that I turned in the loss of our own family children.

Jesus said, "Assuredly, I say to you, unless you are converted and become as little children, you will by no means enter the kingdom of heaven. Therefore whoever humbles himself as this little child is the greatest in the kingdom of heaven. Whoever receives one little child like this in My name receives Me" (Matt. 18:3-5). And then He added this warning in the next verse: "Whoever causes one of these little ones who believe in Me to sin, it would be better for him if a millstone were hung around his neck, and he were drowned in the depth of the sea."

From this passage, it is absolutely clear that God loves and honors children and that He promises a most extreme judgment against those who might lead a child astray.

Jesus expands the Divine perspective on children in the verses following, and this is where I have found my own personal consolation: "Take heed that you do not despise one of these little ones, for I say to you that in heaven their angels always see the face of My Father who is in heaven. For the Son of Man has come to save that which was lost. What do you think? If a man has a hundred sheep, and one of them goes astray, does he not leave the ninety-nine and go to the mountains to seek the one that is straying? And if he should find it, assuredly, I say to you, he rejoices more over that sheep than over the ninety-nine that did not go astray. Even so it is not the will of your Father who is in heaven that one of these little ones should perish" (Matt. 18:10-14).

These are truly powerful words of Jesus and they offer special comfort to those who have lost children, both before and after birth. And for those who seek it, there is that same comfort promised by Jesus and confirmed by the "Comforter, the Holy Spirit" to those who have lost loved ones of any age.

In 2 Corinthians 1:3 the apostle Paul wrote, "Blessed be God, even the Father of our Lord Jesus Christ, the Father of mercies and the God of all comfort...."

To lose a child is devastating to loving parents. Yet God is there to walk with them through such a difficult time, because He understands and cares, since, after all He witnessed the death of His own Son on the Cross. Yet through that loss He made it possible for us to have hope of reunion with those who have gone before us, including our children, for as the Psalmist David said, on the hearing of the death of his own newborn son, "Can I bring him back again? I shall go to him, but he shall not return to me" (2 Sam. 12: 23).

Conclusion

This brings us to the end of this study and as you see, we have come full circle in the story of life and its connection to "Faith."

If can be summed up by words from 1 Corinthians 15:12-20, "Now if Christ is preached that He has been raised from the dead, how do some among you say that there is no resurrection of the dead? But if there is no resurrection of the dead, then Christ is not risen. And if Christ is not risen, then our preaching is empty and your faith is also empty. Yes, and we are found false witnesses of God, because we have testified of God that He raised up Christ, whom He did not raise up—if in fact the dead do not rise. For if the dead do not rise, then Christ is not risen. And if Christ is not risen, your faith is futile; you are still in your sins! Then also those who have fallen asleep in Christ have perished. If in this life only we have hope in Christ, we are of all men the most pitiable."

To this, the apostle Paul adds: "But now Christ is risen from the dead, and has become the firstfruits of those who have fallen asleep. For since by man came death, by Man also came the resurrection of the dead. For as in Adam all die, even so in Christ all shall be made alive. But each one in his own order: Christ the firstfruits, afterward those who are Christ's at His coming. Then comes the end, when He delivers the kingdom to God the Father, when He puts an end to all rule and all authority and power. For He must reign till He has put all enemies under His feet. The last enemy that will be destroyed is death....

"Behold, I tell you a mystery: We shall not all sleep, but we shall all be changed — in a moment, in the twinkling of an eye, at the last trumpet. For the trumpet will sound, and the dead will be raised incorruptible, and we shall be changed. For this corruptible must put on incorruption, and this mortal must put on immortality. So when this corruptible has put on incorruption, and this mortal has put on immortality, then shall be brought to pass the saying that is written: 'Death is swallowed up in victory.'

"O Death, where is your sting? O Hades, where is your victory?

"The sting of death is sin, and the strength of sin is the law. But thanks be to God, who gives us the victory through our Lord Jesus Christ. Therefore, my beloved brethren, be steadfast, immovable, always abounding in the work of the Lord, knowing that your labor is not in vain in the Lord."

If in the end, we take away all the trappings associated with Christianity, what do we have? Without all the religious names we choose, the gowns, the hats, the icons, the traditions, the symbols, the elaborate buildings, the feasts, the rules, and a million other things! What do we have?

What we have is JESUS pure and simple! We have His life, teaching, death, burial, resurrection and coming again! That is what we should have and that is what makes our "faith" real. When we lay down for the last time, will that be it? Or will you have the assurance of eternal life, through faith in Christ, as the apostle John put it, "These things I have written to you who believe in the name of the Son of God, *that you may know that you have eternal life*, and that you may continue to believe in the name of the Son of God" (1 Jn. 5.13, italics added for emphasis).

NOTES

NOTES

NOTES

Resources from Healthy Life Press

Unless otherwise noted on the site itself, shipping is free for all products purchased through *www.healthylifepress.com*.

New Releases – Fall 2014

Mommy, What's 'Died' Mean? - How the Butterfly Story Helped Little Dave Understand His Grandpa's Death, by Linda Swain Gill; Illustrated by David Lee Bass (a.k.a. "Little Dave") – Designed to assist Christian parents and other adults who love and care about children to talk with them about the difficult subject of death, the story traces a small child's experience following his grandpa's and shows how his mother sensitively answered his questions about death by using simple examples derived from the birth of a butterfly. Little Dave's story is colorfully illustrated and designed for a child and parent or trusted adult to read together. The story has been created especially for children from pre-kindergarten through 4th grade. Discussion questions are included for each story page to help determine how much the child understands. A simple imitation game is also included to help involve the child in the story. Several pages at the end of the book contain suggestions about how to discuss death and dying with children of various ages. (**Full-color printed book:** $14.99; PDF eBook: $9.99; both together: $19.99 – direct from publisher; printed books and eBooks available at *www.Amazon.com*; *www.BN.com*; *www.deepershopping.com*, and wherever books are sold.)

No Worries - Spiritual and Mental Health Counseling for Anxiety, by Elaine Leong Eng, MD – Offering a unique spiritual and mental health perspective on a major malady of our age, this practicing Christian psychiatrist has packed a dose of reality mixed with medicine and faith into a book aimed at informing, inspiring, and equipping those who wish to better help those who struggle with anxiety and related disorders, both inside and outside the church. As one endorser said, "I travel all over the world. I see fellow believers suffering from different forms of anxiety and worry. Dr. Eng's book gives me tools to recognize when people are suffering and how to encourage them to get the help they need." (Printed book: $19.99; PDF eBook: $9.99; both together: $24.99 – direct from publisher; printed books and eBooks available at *www.Amazon.com*; *www.BN. com*; *www.deepershopping.com*, and wherever books are sold.)

If God Is So Good, Why Do I Hurt So Bad?, by David B. Biebel, DMin – This **25th Anniversary Edition** of a best-selling classic (over 200,000 copies in print worldwide, in a dozen languages) is the book's first major revision since its initial release in 1989. This new version features additional original material related to the conundrum of suffering and faith (with principles learned along the way), and chapter ending questions for personal or group use. Endorser Sheila Walsh wrote, "I believe this is one of the most profound, empathetic and beautiful books ever written on the subject of suffering and loss. There is no attempt to quickly ease our pain but rather, with an understanding born in the crucible God uniquely designed for him, David offers a place to stand, a place to fall and a place to rise again. This book left an indelible mark on my heart over twenty years ago and now with this new release the gift is fresh and fragrant. I highly commend this to you!" (Printed book: $14.99; PDF eBook: $9.99; both together: $19.95 – direct from publisher; printed books and eBooks available at *www.Amazon.com*; *www.BN.com*; *www. deepershopping.com*, and wherever books are sold.)

"In this remarkable book, my friend Dave Biebel helps the reader understand exactly what's so good about God in the midst of suffering."   – Joni Eareckson Tada

For information on how to publish with us, contact us at: *info@healthylifepress.com*.

EARLIER RELEASES

We've Got Mail: The New Testament Letters in Modern English – As Relevant Today as Ever! by Rev. Warren C. Biebel, Jr. – A modern English paraphrase of the New Testament Letters, sure to inspire in readers a loving appreciation for God's Word. (Printed book: $9.95; PDF eBook: $6.95; both together: $15.00 – direct from publisher; printed books and eBooks available at *www.Amazon.com*; *www.BN.com*; *www.deepershopping. com*, and wherever books are sold.)

Hearth & Home – Recipes for Life, by Karey Swan (7th Edition) – Far more than a cookbook, this classic is a life book, with recipes for life as well as for great food. Karey describes how to buy and prepare from scratch a wide variety of tantalizing dishes, while weaving into the book's fabric the wisdom of the ages plus the recipe that she and her husband used to raise their kids. A great gift for Christmas or for a new bride. (Perfect Bound book [8 x 10, glossy cover]: $17.95; PDF eBook: $12.95; both together: $24.95 – direct from publisher; printed books and eBooks available at *www.Amazon.com*; *www.BN.com*; *www.deepershopping.com*, and wherever books are sold.)

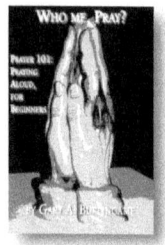

Who Me, Pray? Prayer 101: Praying Aloud, for Beginners, by Gary A. Burlingame – Who Me, Pray? is a practical guide for prayer, based on Jesus' direction in "The Lord's Prayer," with examples provided for use in typical situations where you might be asked or expected to pray in public. (Printed book: $6.95; PDF eBook: $2.99; both together: $7.95 – direct from publisher; printed books and eBooks available at *www.Amazon.com*; *www.BN. com*; *www.deepershopping.com*, and wherever books are sold.)

My Broken Heart Sings, the poetry of Gary Burlingame – In 1987, Gary and his wife Debbie lost their son Christopher John, at only six months of age, to a chronic lung disease. This life-changing experience gave them a special heart for helping others through similar loss and pain. (Printed book: $10.95; PDF eBook: $6.95; both together: $13.95 – direct from publisher; printed books and eBooks available at *www.Amazon.com*; *www. BN.com*; *www.deepershopping.com*, and wherever books are sold.)

After Normal: One Teen's Journey Following Her Brother's Death, by Diane Aggen – Based on a journal the author kept following her younger brother's death. It offers helpful insights and understanding for teens facing a similar loss or for those who might wish to understand and help teens facing a similar loss. (Printed book: $11.95; PDF eBook: $6.95; both together: $15.00 – direct from publisher; printed books and eBooks available at *www.Amazon.com*; *www.BN.com*; *www.deepershopping.com*, and wherever books are sold.)

In the Unlikely Event of a Water Landing – Lessons Learned from Landing in the Hudson River, by Andrew Jamison, MD – The author was flying standby on US Airways Flight 1549 toward Charlotte on January 15, 2009, from New York City, where he had been interviewing for a residency position. Little did he know that the next stop would be the Hudson River. Riveting and inspirational, this book would be especially helpful for people in need of hope and encouragement. (Printed book: $8.95; PDF eBook: $6.95; both together: $12.95 – direct from publisher; printed books and eBooks available at *www.Amazon.com*; *www.BN.com*; *www.deepershopping.com*, and wherever books are sold.)

Finding Martians in the Dark – Everything I Needed to Know About Teaching Took Me Only 30 Years to Learn, by Dan M. Biebel – Packed with wise advice based on hard experience, and laced with humor, this book is a perfect teacher's gift year-round. Susan J. Wegmann, PhD, says, "Biebel's sardonic wit is mellowed by a genuine love for kids and teaching. . . . A Whitman-like sensibility flows through his stories of teaching, learning, and life." (Printed book: $10.95; PDF eBook: $6.95; Together: $15.00 – direct from publisher; printed books and eBooks available at *www.Amazon.com*; *www.BN.com*; *www.deepershopping.com*, and wherever books are sold.)

Because We're Family and **Because We're Friends**, by Gary A. Burlingame – Sometimes things related to faith can be hard to discuss with your family and friends. These booklets are designed to be given as gifts, to help you open the door to discussing spiritual matters with family members and friends who are open to such a conversation. (Printed book: $5.95 each; PDF eBook: $4.95 each; both together: $9.95 [printed & eBook of the same title] – direct from publisher; printed books and eBooks available at *www.Amazon.com*; *www.BN.com*; *www.deepershopping.com*, and wherever books are sold.)

The Transforming Power of Story: How Telling Your Story Brings Hope to Others and Healing to Yourself, by Elaine Leong Eng, MD, and David B. Biebel, DMin – This book demonstrates, through multiple true life stories, how sharing one's story, especially in a group setting, can bring hope to listeners and healing to the one who shares. Individuals facing difficulties will find this book greatly encouraging. (Printed book: $14.99; PDF eBook: $9.99; both together: $19.99 – direct from

publisher; printed books and eBooks available at *www.Amazon.com*; *www.BN.com*; *www.deepershopping.com*, and wherever books are sold.)

You Deserved a Better Father: Good Parenting Takes a Plan, by Robb Brandt, MD – About parenting by intention, and other lessons the author learned through the loss of his firstborn son. It is especially for parents who believe that bits and pieces of leftover time will be enough for their own children. (Printed book: $12.95 each; PDF eBook: $6.95; both together: $17.95 – direct from publisher; printed books and eBooks available at *www.Amazon.com*; *www.BN.com*; *www.deepershopping.com*, and wherever books are sold.)

Jonathan, You Left Too Soon, by David B. Biebel, DMin – One pastor's journey through the loss of his son, into the darkness of depression, and back into the light of joy again, emerging with a renewed sense of mission. (Printed book: $12.95; PDF eBook: $5.99; both together: $15.00 – direct from publisher; printed books and eBooks available at *www.Amazon.com*; *www.BN.com*; *www.deepershopping.com*, and wherever books are sold.)

Printed Cover | eBook Cover

The Spiritual Fitness Checkup for the 50-Something Woman, by Sharon V. King, PhD – Following the stages of a routine medical exam, the author describes ten spiritual fitness "checkups" midlife women can conduct to assess their spiritual health and tone up their relationship with God. Each checkup consists of the author's personal reflections, a Scripture reference for meditation, and a "Spiritual Pulse Check," with exercises readers can use for personal application. (Printed book: $8.95; PDF eBook: $6.95; both together: $12.95 – direct from publisher; printed books and eBooks available at *www.Amazon.com*; *www.BN.com*; *www.deepershopping.com*, and wherever books are sold.)

The Other Side of Life – Over 60? God Still Has a Plan for You, by Rev. Warren C. Biebel, Jr. – Drawing on biblical examples and his 60-plus years of pastoral experience, Rev. Biebel helps older (and younger) adults understand God's view of aging and the rich life available to everyone who seeks a deeper relationship with God as they age. Rev. Biebel explains how to: Identify God's ongoing plan for your life; Rely on faith to manage the anxieties of aging; Form positive, supportive relationships; Cultivate patience; Cope with new technologies; Develop spiritual integrity; Understand the effects of dementia; Develop a Christ-centered perspective of aging. (Printed book: $10.95; PDF eBook: $6.95; both together: $15.00 – direct from publisher; printed books and eBooks available at *www.Amazon.com*; *www.BN.com*; *www.deepershopping.com*, and wherever books are sold.)

My Faith, My Poetry, by Gary A. Burlingame – This unique book of Christian poetry is actually two in one. The first collection of poems, A Day in the Life, explores a working parent's daily journey of faith. The reader is carried from morning to bedtime, from "In the Details," to "I Forgot to Pray," back to "Home Base," and finally to "Eternal Love Divine." The second collection of poems, Come Running, is wonder, joy, and faith wrapped up in words that encourage and inspire the mind and the heart. (Printed book: $10.95; PDF eBook: $6.95; both together: $13.95 – direct from publisher; printed books and eBooks available at *www.Amazon.com*; *www.BN.com*; *www.deepershopping.com*, and wherever books are sold.)

On Eagles' Wings, by Sara Eggleston – One woman's life journey from idyllic through chaotic to joy, carried all the way by the One who has promised to never leave us nor forsake us. Remarkable, poignant, moving, and inspiring, this autobiographical account will help many who are facing difficulties that seem too great to overcome or even bear at all. It is proof that Isaiah 40:31 is

as true today as when it was penned, "But they that wait upon the LORD shall renew their strength; they shall mount up with wings as eagles; they shall run, and not be weary; and they shall walk, and not faint." (Printed book: $14.95; PDF eBook: $8.95; both together: $22.95 – direct from publisher; printed books and eBooks available at *www.Amazon.com*; *www. BN.com*; *www.deepershopping.com*, and wherever books are sold.)

Richer Descriptions, by Gary A. Burlingame – A unique and handy manual, covering all nine human senses in seven chapters, for Christian speakers and writers. Exercises and a speaker's checklist equip speakers to engage their audiences in a richer experience. Writing examples and a writer's guide help writers bring more life to the characters and scenes of their stories. Bible references encourage a deeper appreciation of being created by God for a sensory existence. (Printed book: $15.95; PDF eBook: $8.95; both together: $22.95 – direct from publisher; printed books and eBooks available at *www.Amazon.com*; *www.BN.com*; *www.deepershopping.com*, and wherever books are sold.)

Treasuring Grace, by Rob Plumley and Tracy Roberts – This novel was inspired by a dream. Liz Swanson's life isn't quite what she'd imagined, but she considers herself lucky. She has a good husband, beautiful children, and fulfillment outside of her home through volunteer work. On some days she doesn't even notice the dull ache in her heart. While she's preparing for their summer kickoff at Lake George,  the ache disappears and her sudden happiness is mistaken for anticipation of their weekend. However, as the family heads north, there are clouds on the horizon that have nothing to do with the weather. Only Liz's daughter, who's found some of her mother's hidden journals, has any idea what's wrong. But by the end of the weekend, there will be no escaping the truth or its painful buried secrets. (Printed: $12.95; PDF eBook: $7.95; both together: $19.95 – direct from publisher; printed books and eBooks available at *www.Amazon.com*; *www.BN.com*; *www.deepershopping.com*, and wherever books are sold.)

From Orphan to Physician – The Winding Path, by Chun-Wai Chan, MD – From the foreword: "In this book, Dr. Chan describes how his family escaped to Hong Kong, how they survived in utter poverty, and how he went from being an orphan to graduating from Harvard Medical School and becoming a cardiologist. The writing is fluent, easy to read and understand. The sequence of events is realistic, emotionally moving, spiritually touching, heart-warming, and thought provoking. The book illustrates . . . how one must have faith in order to walk through life's winding path." (Printed book: $14.95; PDF eBook: $8.95; both together: $22.95 – direct from publisher; printed books and eBooks available at *www.Amazon.com*; *www.BN.com*; *www.deepershopping.com*, and wherever books are sold.)

12 Parables, by Wayne Faust – Timeless Christian stories about doubt, fear, change, grief, and more. Using tight, entertaining prose, professional musician and comedy performer Wayne Faust manages to deal with difficult concepts in a simple, straightforward way. These are stories you can read aloud over and over— to your spouse, your family, or in a group setting. Packed with emotion and just enough mystery to keep you wondering, while providing lots of points to ponder and discuss when you're through, these stories relate the gospel in the tradition of the greatest speaker of parables the world has ever known, who appears in them often. (Printed book: $14.95; PDF eBook: $8.95; both together: $22.95 – direct from publisher; printed books and eBooks available at *www.Amazon.com*; *www.BN.com*; *www.deepershopping.com*, and wherever books are sold.)

Unless otherwise noted on the site itself, shipping is free for all products purchased through <u>www.healthylifepress.com</u>.

The Answer is Always "Jesus," by Aram Haroutunian, who gave children's sermons for 15 years at a large church in Golden, Colorado—well over 500 in all. This book contains 74 of his most unforgettable presentations—due to the children's responses. Pastors, homeschoolers, parents who often lead family devotions, or other storytellers will find these stories, along with comments about props and how to prepare and present them, an invaluable asset in reconnecting with the simplest, most profound truths of Scripture, and then to envision how best to communicate these so even a child can understand them. (Printed book: $12.95; PDF eBook: $8.95; both together: $19.95 – direct from publisher; printed books and eBooks available at *www.Amazon.com*; *www.BN.com*; *www.deepershopping.com*, and wherever books are sold.)

Handbook of Faith, by Rev. Warren C. Biebel, Jr. – The New York Times World 2011 Almanac claimed that there are 2 billion, 200 thousand Christians in the world, with "Christians" being defined as "followers of Christ." The original 12 followers of Christ changed the world; indeed, they changed the history of the world. So this author, a pastor with over 60 years' experience, poses and answers this logical question: "If there are so many 'Christians' on this planet, why are they so relatively ineffective in serving the One they claim to follow?" Answer: Because, unlike Him, they do not know and trust the Scriptures, implicitly. This little volume will help you do that. (Printed book: $8.95; PDF eBook: $6.95; both together: $13.95 – direct from publisher; printed books and eBooks available at *www.Amazon.com*; *www.BN.com*; *www.deepershopping.com*, and wherever books are sold.)

For information about how to publish with us, contact us at: info@healthylifepress.com.

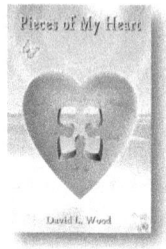

Pieces of My Heart, by David L. Wood – Eighty-two lessons from normal everyday life. David's hope is that these stories will spark thoughts about God's constant involvement and intervention in our lives and stir a sense of how much He cares about every detail that is important to us. The piece missing represents his son, Daniel, who died in a fire shortly before his first birthday. (Printed book: $16.95; PDF eBook: $8.95; both together: $24.95 – direct from publisher; printed books and eBooks available at *www.Amazon.com*; *www.BN.com*; *www.deepershopping.com*, and wherever books are sold.)

Dream House, by Justa Carpenter – Written by a New England builder of several hundred homes, the idea for this book came to him one day as he was driving that came to him one day as was driving from one job site to another. He pulled over and recorded it so he would remember it, and now you will remember it, too, if you believe, as he does, that ". . . He who has begun a good work in you will complete it until the day of Jesus Christ." (Printed book: $10.95; PDF eBook: $6.95; both together: $13.95 – direct from publisher; printed books and eBooks available at *www.Amazon.com*; *www.BN.com*; *www.deepershopping.com*, and wherever books are sold.)

A Simply Homemade Clean, by homesteader Lisa Barthuly – "Somewhere along the path, it seems we've lost our gumption, the desire to make things ourselves," says the author. "Gone are the days of 'do it yourself.' Really . . . why bother? There are a slew of retailers just waiting for us with anything and everything we could need; packaged up all pretty, with no thought or effort required. It is the manifestation of 'progress' . . . right?" I don't buy that!" Instead, Lisa describes how to make safe and effective cleansers for home, laundry, and body right in your own home. This saves money and avoids exposure to harmful chemicals often found in commercially produced cleansers. (**Full-color** printed book: $16.99; PDF eBook: $6.95; both together: $22.95 – direct from publisher; printed books and eBooks available at *www.Amazon.com*; *www.BN.com*; *www.deepershopping.com*, and wherever books are sold.)

The Secret of Singing Springs, by Monte Swan – One Colorado family's treasure-hunting adventure along the trail of Jesse James. The Secret of Singing Springs is written to capture for children and their parents the spirit of the hunt—the hunt for treasure as in God's Truth, which is the objective of walking the Way of Wisdom that is described in Proverbs. (Printed book: $12.95, PDF eBook: $9.99; both together: $19.99 – direct from publisher; printed books and eBooks available at *www.Amazon.com*; *www.BN.com*; *www.deepershopping.com*, and wherever books are sold.)

God Loves You Circle, by Michelle Johnson – Daily inspiration for your deeper walk with Christ. This collection of short stories of Christian living will make you laugh, make you cry, but most of all make you contemplate—the meaning and value of walking with the Master moment-by-moment, day-by-day. (**Full-color** printed book: $17.95; PDF eBook: $9.99; both together: $22.99 – direct from publisher; printed books and eBooks available at *www.Amazon.com*; *www.BN.com*; *www.deepershopping.com*, and wherever books are sold.)

Our God-Given Senses, by Gary A. Burlingame – Did you know humans have NINE senses? The Bible draws on these senses to reveal spiritual truth. We are to taste and see that the Lord is a good. We are to carry the fragrance of Christ. Our faith is produced upon hearing. Jesus asked Thomas to touch him. God created us for a sensory experience and that is what you will find in this book. (Printed book: $12.99; PDF eBook: $9.99; both together: $19.99 – direct from publisher; printed books and eBooks available at *www.Amazon.com*; *www.BN.com*; *www.deepershopping.com*, and wherever books are sold.)

Vows, a Romantic novel by F. F. Whitestone – When the police cruiser pulled up to the curb outside, Faith Framingham's heart skipped a beat, for she could see that Chuck, who should have been driving, was not in the vehicle. Chuck's partner, Sandy, stepped out slowly. Sandy's pursed lips and ashen face spoke volumes. Faith waited by the front door, her hands clasped tightly, to counter the fact that her mind was already reeling. "Love never fails." A compelling story. (Printed book: $12.99; PDF eBook: $9.99; both together, $19.99 – direct from publisher; printed books and eBooks available at *www.Amazon.com*; *www.BN.com*; *www.deepershopping.com*, and wherever books are sold.)

Worth the Cost?, by Jack Tsai, MD – The author was happily on his way to obtaining the American Dream until he decided to take seriously Jesus' command, "Come, follow me." Join him as he explores the cost of medical education and Christian discipleship. Planning to serve God in your future vocation? Take care that your desires do not get side-tracked by the false promises of this world. What you should be doing now so when you are done with your training you will still want to serve God. (Printed book: $12.99, PDF eBook: $9.99; both together: $19.99 – direct from publisher; printed books and eBooks available at *www.Amazon.com*; *www. BN.com*; *www.deepershopping.com*, and wherever books are sold.)

Nature: God's Second Book – An Essential Link to Restoring Your Personal Health and Wellness: Body, Mind, and Spirit, by Elvy P. Rolle – An inspirational book that looks at nature across the seasons of nature and of life. It uses the biblical Emmaus Journey as an analogy for life's journey, and offers ideas for using nature appreciation and exploration to reduce life's stresses. The author shares her personal story of how she came to grips with this concept after three trips to the emergency room. (**Full-color** printed book: $12.99; PDF eBook $8.99; both together: $16.99 – direct from publisher; printed books and eBooks available at *www.Amazon.com*; *www.BN.com*; *www.deepershopping.com*, and wherever books are sold.)

He Waited, by LaDonna Cooper – Inspires readers to wait upon the Lord for His best for them; stresses the importance of putting God's purpose above one's own; emphasizes that God's love is unconditional; demonstrates the wisdom of waiting, through a combination of positive insights, encouragement, biblical examples and principles. Decorated with original poetry by the author. For singles and others who are waiting. Distributed primarily through *www.Amazon.com*. (Printed book: $10.99; PDF eBook: $9.99; both together: $15.99 – direct from publisher; printed books and eBooks available at *www.Amazon.com*; *www.BN.com*; *www.deepershopping.com*, and wherever books are sold.)

Seasonal

The Big Black Book – What the Christmas Tree Saw, by Rev. Warren C. Biebel, Jr. – An original Christmas story, from the perspective of the Christmas tree. This little book is especially suitable for parents to read to their children at Christmas time or all year-round. (**Full-color** printed book: $9.95; PDF eBook: $4.95; both together: $12.95 – direct from publisher; printed books and eBooks available at *www.Amazon.com*; *www.BN.com*; *www.deepershopping.com*, and wherever books are sold.)

www.ingramcontent.com/pod-product-compliance
Lightning Source LLC
Chambersburg PA
CBHW052105070526
44584CB00017B/2337